Understanding the Elements of the Periodic Table™

HYDROGEN

Linda Saucerman

rosen central™

The Rosen Publishing Group, Inc., New York

To Steve Saucerman

Published in 2005 by The Rosen Publishing Group, Inc.
29 East 21st Street, New York, NY 10010

Library of Congress Cataloging-in-Publication Data

Saucerman, Linda.
Hydrogen / by Linda Saucerman.—
      p. cm.—(Understanding the Elements of the Periodic Table)
Summary: Explains the characteristics of hydrogen, where it is found, how it is used by humans, and its relationship to other elements found in the periodic table. Includes bibliographical references and index.
ISBN 1-4042-0156-4 (library binding.)
1. Hydrogen—Juvenile literature. [1. Hydrogen. 2. Periodic laws—Tables.]
I. Title. II. Series.
QD181.H1S16 2004
546'.21—dc22

2003022261

On the cover: Hydrogen's square on the periodic table of elements. Inset: The atomic structure of hydrogen

Manufactured in the United States of America

Contents

Introduction

May 6, 1937, was no ordinary day for the town of Lakehurst, New Jersey. What began as a day filled with happiness and excitement in this quaint town ended in tragedy like no one had seen before. The events that unfolded on this day would contribute to Lakehurst's motto, "A small town with a big history."

It was on this day that the famous *Hindenburg* blimp was to land in Lakehurst after making a trip from Germany and crossing the Atlantic Ocean. Larger than the *Titanic* and the length of three football fields, the *Hindenburg* was the largest airship ever. Built during Adolf Hitler's reign of power, this immense blimp featured gigantic Nazi swastikas on its tail fins. If all went well, the *Hindenburg* would be used for luxury travel to and from America and Europe, becoming the first transatlantic commercial airliner.

The blimp could travel 84 miles per hour (135 kilometers per hour) and carry nearly 100 people. It had a dining room and reading areas. It even had a smoking lounge, which seems a bit foolish considering that the blimp was filled with hydrogen, a highly flammable gas that is lighter than air.

Despite a thunderstorm in New Jersey that day, the *Hindenburg* flight seemed to be going well. A large crowd had gathered to watch

On May 6, 1937, the fury of the elements was released when the *Hindenburg* exploded in a horrific accident, claiming the lives of thirty-six people. The airship was kept aloft by hydrogen, an elemental gas. Colorless and odorless, hydrogen is extremely flammable—a simple spark caused the hydrogen-filled *Hindenburg* to burst into flames.

the colossal blimp make its landing, and newspaper and radio news reporters were present to cover the big event.

But as the massive airship began to make its descent over Lakehurst, something went horribly wrong. A fire suddenly appeared at the stern, or back, of the blimp. The airship burst into flames. Thirty-two seconds after the first flame was spotted, the *Hindenburg* crashed to the ground. The crowd of onlookers frantically scrambled for safety and rescuers ran to help. A Chicago radio reporter was so shocked by what he saw that he could not control his emotions. The reporter shouted into his microphone the events that were happening. He described how the *Hindenburg* was all smoke and fire and anxiously told the spectators to get out of harm's way. At one point, he cried out, "Oh, the humanity!" as he watched the *Hindenburg* become engulfed in flames. His report of the incident was broadcast all over the world, and "Oh, the humanity" became a famous quote that, to this day, expresses tragedy.

In the end, thirty-six people died from the crash. Some say an electrical spark from the storm clouds caused the thin skin of the *Hindenburg* to ignite, while others say the spark ignited the hydrogen. Although the cause is still debatable, blimps, hot air balloons, and other airships now use safer, nonflammable helium to get their lift.

For the history of hydrogen, however, the *Hindenburg*'s tragic trip drove home the knowledge that hydrogen, the universe's lightest element, is also one of the most dangerous.

Chapter One
Henry's Hydrogen

While hydrogen is related to one of the most fantastic tragedies of the modern world, the element is also prized because it is considered responsible for life on Earth. We can literally thank our lucky stars for hydrogen. Without it, there would be no stars in the night sky and no sunshine. Hydrogen is an element that is considered to be one of the building blocks of all life. Hydrogen makes it possible for planet Earth, its water, its soil, and all life—including you and me—to exist.

So, if hydrogen is invisible, how do we know it is there? Although hydrogen is odorless, colorless, and tasteless, it's possible to determine that it exists. The man who first discovered hydrogen was Henry Cavendish, a very rich, very smart, and very odd scientist from London. He was so shy that he could hardly talk to people, and he never spoke to women. In fact, he would leave handwritten instructions to his maid and other female servants instead of talking to them.

One day in 1766, Cavendish was experimenting with zinc (known as Zn in the periodic table of elements) and a fuming, poisonous acid. When he mixed the two together, they created a gas he called "inflammable air." He realized that this new substance contained its own properties and should be considered an element. An

English chemist Henry Cavendish was the first person to identify the element hydrogen, but he mistakenly dubbed the new element "inflammable air." Cavendish also discovered that water is not an element. Rather, it is a compound consisting of hydrogen and oxygen (O).

element is matter from which all things in the universe are made. But it wasn't until 1787, when another scientist, Antoine-Laurent Lavoisier of France, gave this inflammable air the name hydrogen. The name comes from the Greek words *hydro*, meaning "water," and *genes* (pronounced "GEN-us"), meaning "generator." You'll learn why this element is a water generator in chapter two.

The Anatomy of Atoms

After hydrogen was discovered, scientists realized that hydrogen is the simplest of all atoms and that it also is the most prevalent, or widespread.

All elements are made up of atoms. In fact, each element is made up of only one kind of atom: what changes is just how many atoms. So, whether you have one atom of gold, or a nugget made up of many atoms of pure gold, you still have just one element—gold (Au).

No two elements are exactly alike. This is because of their atoms. Atoms unite with other atoms to form a molecule. A molecule is two or more atoms that are chemically bound together in a fixed ratio, or number. A fixed combination of atoms will create different hydrogen

Henry Cavendish

The discovery of what became known as hydrogen wasn't Henry Cavendish's only claim to fame. His work made him a pioneer in the study of gases, and he determined ways to collect and store them in bottles for further research. Through such research, he was able to determine that three main elements combine to make the air we breathe. Although he did not use the names of the elements that make up air, he was right in realizing that there were three main substances in air. These were later identified as nitrogen (N), argon (Ar), and oxygen (O).

Cavendish's other famous discovery took place between 1796 and 1798, when he established that the average density of Earth was 5.448 kg/m^3. His numbers were not that far off from the 5.5 kg/m^3 that scientists currently say is the estimated average density of Earth.

molecules. One hydrogen atom is called atomic hydrogen (H). Hydrogen gas (H$_2$), or molecular hydrogen, is made of two hydrogen atoms bound together to make a diatomic molecule.

The most important particles that make up atoms are subatomic particles known as protons, neutrons, and electrons. Protons have a positive electric charge, neutrons have no charge, and electrons have a negative electric charge. All atoms contain a nucleus, or center, where the protons and neutrons are contained. Outside of the nucleus are shells that contain the electrons. The first shell can hold only two electrons, the second shell can hold up to eight, and the third shell can hold up to eighteen. An atom can have up to seven shells of electrons.

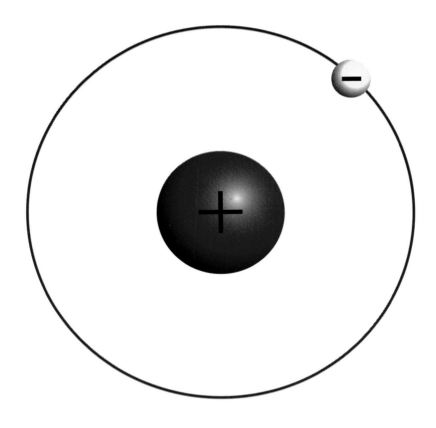

Hydrogen is the lightest and simplest of all elements in the periodic table. One hydrogen atom contains only a nucleus with one proton and no neutrons Only one negatively charged electron orbits, or circles, the nucleus.

Looking at the atomic makeup of hydrogen, you'll see that hydrogen has only one proton, one electron, and no neutrons. (Isotopes of hydrogen, discussed in chapter three, have different numbers of neutrons.) The number of protons and the number of electrons are almost always equal. The number of protons is called the atomic number, and no two elements have the same atomic number. The periodic table of elements is organized according to the atomic numbers of elements, from the lowest to the highest. Hydrogen has an atomic number of 1, so it is listed as the first element on the periodic table. The periodic table has more than 100 elements, with 92 found naturally and the rest man-made. Hydrogen is mostly found in the form of a gas, and its chemical symbol on the periodic table is H.

In addition to having just one proton, hydrogen also has the lowest atomic weight (relative atomic mass) of all the elements. It weighs in

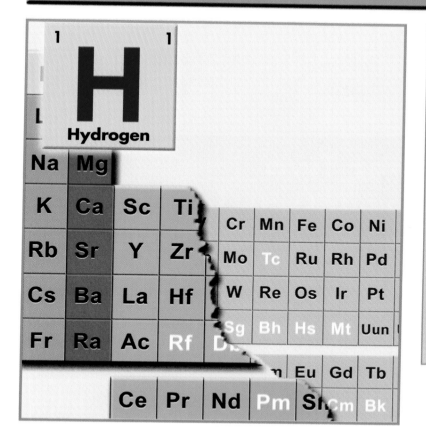

Hydrogen sits atop the periodic table of elements. Because it contains only one proton and one electron, hydrogen's atomic number is 1. While hydrogen is not the most common element found on Earth, it is the most common element in the universe. The Sun is about 92 percent hydrogen. The remaining 8 percent is helium.

at 1.00794 atomic mass units. The atomic weight is the mass of one atom of the element. Now that we know that hydrogen is the most abundant and lightest element, let's look at its number one position on the periodic table.

Chapter Two
Hydrogen Gets Top Billing

Russian chemist Dmitry Mendeleyev first published his version of the periodic table in 1869. At the time, Mendeleyev was working as a professor at the University of St. Petersburg in Russia. He wanted a method that would help his students understand the relationship between the elements. His solution was the periodic table of elements.

In Mendeleyev's original version, he placed the elements in horizontal rows according to their atomic mass. Not all the elements that we know today had been discovered during Mendeleyev's time. (In fact, more than fifty elements have been added to the table since 1871.) The periodic table we use today has been slightly altered since Mendeleyev's original. The original version arranged the elements according to atomic mass. Today's version orders the elements by atomic number, which is the number of protons in the atom. For hydrogen, though, arranging it by atomic mass or atomic number doesn't make a difference. Hydrogen's atomic weight and atomic number are both 1.

Elements are then organized into periods and groups. Periods are horizontal rows in the table. In each period, elements are arranged by increasing atomic number, reading from left to right. Since hydrogen's atomic weight is 1, it sits in the upper-left corner of the table.

Groups are assigned by the number of electrons found in the outermost shell of the atom. The number of the group appears above

Hydrogen Snapshot

Chemical Symbol:	H
Properties:	Colorless, odorless, tasteless, and extremely flammable
Discovered By:	Henry Cavendish, England, 1766
Atomic Number:	1
Atomic Weight:	1.00794 atomic mass units
Protons:	1
Electrons:	1
Neutrons:	0
Density at 273 K:	0.0899 g/L at 1atm
Melting Point:	14.025 K; -434°F; -258.975°C
Boiling Point:	20.38 K; -422.99°F; -252.77°C
Commonly Found:	Water, air, Earth's crust, Sun, and stars

each column of the table, numbers 1 through 18. All of the elements within a group have similar chemical properties and are sometimes referred to as a "family" of elements. The elements in the A groups are known as representative elements, or elements that can add electrons to their outermost shells. Elements in the B groups are transition elements, or elements that can add electrons to the inner shells of the atom.

Many of the groups of elements have a group name. For example, elements in group IA, where hydrogen is located, are called alkali metals. However, despite its position on the periodic table, hydrogen is an exception in this case and is not considered a metal—it is a nonmetal. Even though hydrogen is in the same group as the alkali metals, the first alkali metal is lithium (Li), followed by sodium (Na), and they continue all the way down to the heaviest alkali metal, francium (Fr). Alkali metals are metals that can combine easily with other elements. Alkalis are also very malleable (they can be extended or shaped by hammering), ductile (they can be pulled into wire), and good conductors of electricity. Alkali metals react violently when they are mixed with water.

Hydrogen is a nonmetal, which is pretty much the opposite of an alkali metal. Nonmetals are not good conductors of electricity, are very brittle, and are not ductile. Nonmetals exist as gases, such as hydrogen, and solids, such as carbon.

Elements in certain groups have similar chemical behaviors because of their electric forces. If you've ever held two magnets together and felt the strong force that makes it impossible for you to stick the two magnets together, then you have an idea of what happens when two protons are near each other. Because protons are positively charged, they repel each other. But it is the negatively charged electrons surrounding the nucleus that really determine how elements behave and react with one another.

Knowing that hydrogen's atomic number is 1, we also know that a single hydrogen atom has just one proton and one electron. Having just one electron makes it easy for this element to combine with other elements

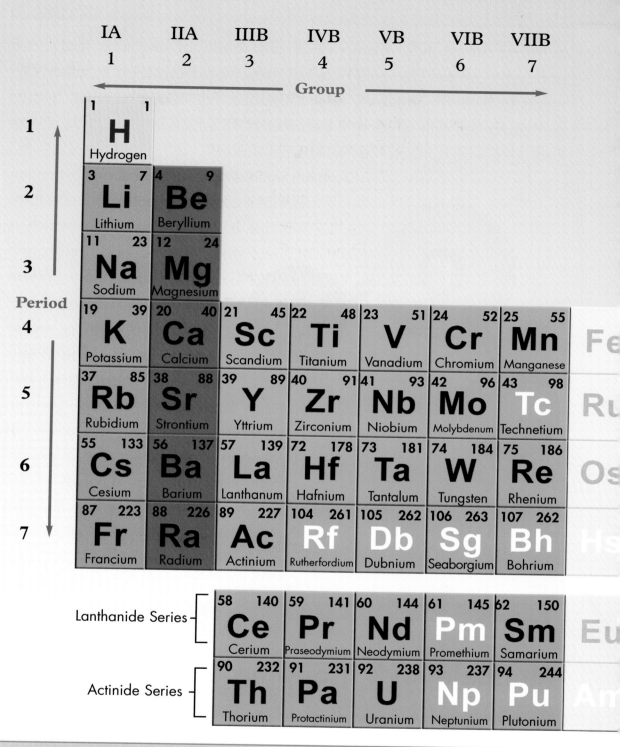

| | IA
1 | IIA
2 | IIIB
3 | IVB
4 | VB
5 | VIB
6 | VIIB
7 |

Group

| Period | | | | | | | |

1 — H ¹/₁ Hydrogen

2 — Li ³/₇ Lithium — Be ⁴/₉ Beryllium

3 — Na ¹¹/₂₃ Sodium — Mg ¹²/₂₄ Magnesium

4 — K ¹⁹/₃₉ Potassium — Ca ²⁰/₄₀ Calcium — Sc ²¹/₄₅ Scandium — Ti ²²/₄₈ Titanium — V ²³/₅₁ Vanadium — Cr ²⁴/₅₂ Chromium — Mn ²⁵/₅₅ Manganese — Fe

5 — Rb ³⁷/₈₅ Rubidium — Sr ³⁸/₈₈ Strontium — Y ³⁹/₈₉ Yttrium — Zr ⁴⁰/₉₁ Zirconium — Nb ⁴¹/₉₃ Niobium — Mo ⁴²/₉₆ Molybdenum — Tc ⁴³/₉₈ Technetium — Ru

6 — Cs ⁵⁵/₁₃₃ Cesium — Ba ⁵⁶/₁₃₇ Barium — La ⁵⁷/₁₃₉ Lanthanum — Hf ⁷²/₁₇₈ Hafnium — Ta ⁷³/₁₈₁ Tantalum — W ⁷⁴/₁₈₄ Tungsten — Re ⁷⁵/₁₈₆ Rhenium — Os

7 — Fr ⁸⁷/₂₂₃ Francium — Ra ⁸⁸/₂₂₆ Radium — Ac ⁸⁹/₂₂₇ Actinium — Rf ¹⁰⁴/₂₆₁ Rutherfordium — Db ¹⁰⁵/₂₆₂ Dubnium — Sg ¹⁰⁶/₂₆₃ Seaborgium — Bh ¹⁰⁷/₂₆₂ Bohrium — Hs

Lanthanide Series — Ce ⁵⁸/₁₄₀ Cerium — Pr ⁵⁹/₁₄₁ Praseodymium — Nd ⁶⁰/₁₄₄ Neodymium — Pm ⁶¹/₁₄₅ Promethium — Sm ⁶²/₁₅₀ Samarium — Eu

Actinide Series — Th ⁹⁰/₂₃₂ Thorium — Pa ⁹¹/₂₃₁ Protactinium — U ⁹²/₂₃₈ Uranium — Np ⁹³/₂₃₇ Neptunium — Pu ⁹⁴/₂₄₄ Plutonium — Am

Though hydrogen is not a metal, it is placed in group IA with the alkali metals lithium, sodium, potassium, rubidium, cesium, and francium. Hydrogen is part of this group because it tends to act like a metal during chemical reactions. Except for hydrogen, all the members of group IA react violently with water and release hydrogen as a result.

to form compounds. Compounds are made of elements that have bonded together. Elements bond by attaching themselves to other elements to form a completely new substance. For example, when hydrogen combines with oxygen, it becomes H_2O, which is water. This is why hydrogen was dubbed the "water generator."

Another interesting characteristic of hydrogen is that it commonly appears in the form of a diatomic molecule, which is two atoms of hydrogen bonded together. When looking at a chemical formula, hydrogen is represented by H_2. The 2 tells us that there are two hydrogen atoms within every diatomic molecule of hydrogen. Looking at the chemical formula for a water molecule (H_2O), we can see that there are two atoms of hydrogen (one diatomic hydrogen molecule) and one atom of oxygen.

Each atom of hydrogen has only one electron, while the oxygen atom has six electrons in its outer shell, with room for two more electrons. Therefore, two hydrogen atoms give their electrons to the oxygen atom. The bond creates a water molecule (H_2O).

Mendeleyev's Mapping of the Elements

If you want to have a school named after you, you either donate a lot of money to education or you make a major scientific discovery. Dmitry Mendeleyev was not from a wealthy family, so his contribution to learning came in the form of his fantastic chart that would change the field of chemistry—and ultimately lead to a university being named in his honor.

Mendeleyev was born in Siberia, a very cold region in Russia, and was the youngest of fourteen children. After studying and teaching in St. Petersburg, he traveled to Paris to get his Ph.D. (doctor of philosophy). Along the way, he stopped at some salt mines in Poland, and it was there that he first had the notion of what would later become the periodic table. The young Mendeleyev took a look around the salt mines and wondered how sodium, chlorine (Cl), bromine (Br), potassium (K), and other elements present in the mine behaved or reacted with each other. This problem

Chemist Dmitry Mendeleyev designed the periodic table as a way to help his students understand the relationship between the elements. He claimed that the final design of the periodic table came to him during a dream.

stuck with him and presented itself several years later while he was teaching in St. Petersburg. He wanted to develop a way for his students to see properties of elements at a glance and was working on arranging and rearranging the known elements. Some accounts say that the arrangement of the elements by atomic weight came to Mendeleyev in a dream. Whether or not he was sleeping, Mendeleyev's periodic table certainly was an eye-opener for the scientific community when it was presented in 1868 and published the following year.

Mendeleyev's arrangement of the elements has been altered and rearranged as scientists have made new discoveries. But its foundation of providing clarity to a confusing world of elements has withstood the test of time.

An early version of Mendeleyev's periodic table of elements appears on a wall of a technical school in Russia. In his final version, completed in 1871, Mendeleyev left gaps on the table to allow for newly discovered elements. Since 1871, more than fifty elements have been identified and added to the periodic table.

Uut and Uup Get on the Table

In early 2004, scientists from America and Russia announced the creation of two new elements. Both elements are called superheavies because of their heavy atomic mass. Element 113 has been named ununtrium (Uut), while element 115 has been named ununpentium (Uup). However, Uut and Uup will not be given a permanent place on the table yet. The team's work has to be published and other scientists have to confirm the existence of the two new elements.

Chapter Three
Hydrogen's Hiding Places

We now know that hydrogen and oxygen can create water, but how is hydrogen found in the first place? One of the amazing things about hydrogen is that it has been around for a really, really long time. Scientists believe that hydrogen appeared when the universe was first formed. Many scientists believe in the big bang theory. This theory states that around 15 billion years ago, a violent explosion of matter sparked the beginning of the universe as we know it today. It was during this big bang that hydrogen is thought to have come into being. One of the reasons scientists believe this theory is because large amounts of hydrogen can be found floating in space, on Earth, on other planets, and in stars. In fact, the Sun, which is a star, contains massive amounts of hydrogen. It is the burning of the hydrogen that keeps the Sun shining. And, as mentioned in chapter one, hydrogen is the most abundant element of the periodic table. It is everywhere. Out of all of the elements, hydrogen makes up nearly 93 percent of all atoms in the entire universe!

Here on Earth, however, we don't find much hydrogen floating around. This is because hydrogen is so light that Earth's gravity can't hold it, and it floats out of the atmosphere. Other planets with greater gravitational pulls, such as Saturn and Jupiter, have a large amount of hydrogen gas in their atmospheres because it cannot simply float away.

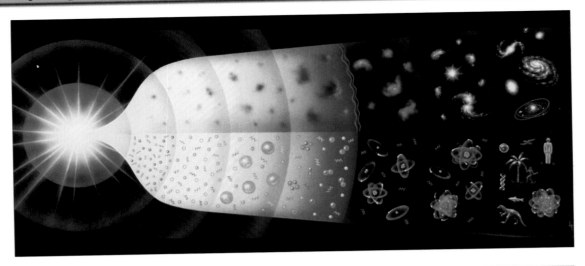

The big bang theory claims that around 15 billion years ago, a violent explosion of matter created the universe, which developed in stages. In the fifth stage, some 300 million years after the big bang, the elements started to form. The seventh stage includes the formation of our solar system and life as we know it today.

Hydrogen Gets Wet

So if there's very little hydrogen in the air, then where is this supposedly abundant element? Usually, hydrogen is found with its buddy oxygen in the form of water in lakes, streams, seas, and our vast oceans. So every time you get a glass of water, take a shower or a bath, or dive into a pool, you are experiencing hydrogen.

If we boil water, will that separate hydrogen from oxygen? No. Boiling water just creates steam, which is the gaseous form of water. However, electrolysis can turn water into hydrogen. Electrolysis is when an electric current runs through a nonmetallic electric conductor such as water. An electric current through water will break the bonds between hydrogen and oxygen, separating the two elements.

Other ways to release hydrogen are through the steam released from heated carbon; the decomposition of certain hydrocarbons (you'll learn

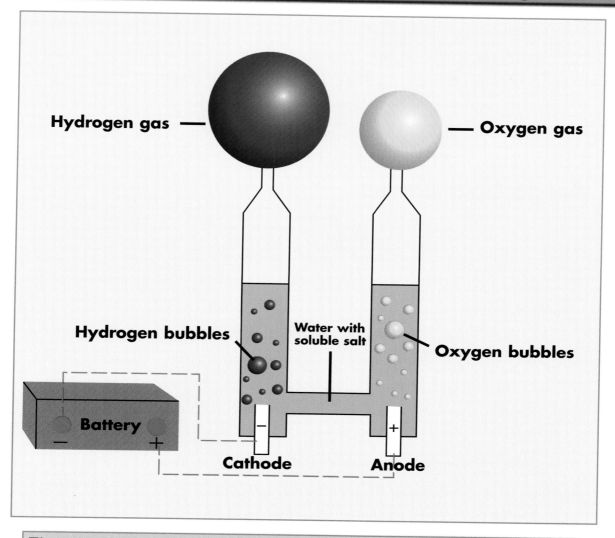

Hydrogen gas — ● — Oxygen gas

Hydrogen bubbles

Water with soluble salt

Oxygen bubbles

Battery

Cathode

Anode

Electrolysis breaks down molecules by using an electric current. A battery will send an electric current through wires and out the negative cathode and positive anode. The electric current then reacts with the water molecules, breaking apart the bonds. The liquid then separates into hydrogen and oxygen gases. Two hydrogen atoms are released for every oxygen molecule.

more about those in chapter four); the reaction of sodium or potassium hydroxide on aluminum; or the displacement (removal) of hydrogen from acids by certain metals. In the United States, these methods to produce hydrogen are used. The hydrogen is then used as a source of energy in nuclear power plants and to fuel spacecraft.

Hydrogen is also found in Earth's crust. But there isn't a lot there—only about 3 percent of the crust is hydrogen. The rest of the crust is made up of oxygen (47 percent), silicon (Si; 28 percent), aluminum (Al; 8 percent), and a variety of other elements, including iron (Fe), calcium (Ca), and sodium (Na).

Acids and Bases

Hydrogen, and especially water, plays an important role in the relationship between groups of chemical compounds called acids and bases. When acids and bases react with each other, they produce completely new substances.

When dissolved in water, acids will produce hydrogen ions. Natural acids are found in fruits, such as lemons, and have a sour taste. For instance, lemons contain a high concentration of citric acid, the chemical that makes your lips pucker. Citric acid is a safe acid, but some acids can burn skin or tissue. Hydrochloric acid (HCl) is a dangerous acid that can be strong enough to corrode metal. However, in a weakened form, hydrochloric acid can be helpful. In fact, a diluted form of hydrochloric acid is found in your stomach and aids in digestion. Other acids are nitric acid (HNO_3), sulfuric acid (H_2SO_4), and perchloric acid ($HClO_4$).

Bases, when dissolved in water, will produce hydroxide ions (OH^-). Some examples of bases are ammonia (NH_3), lithium hydroxide (LiOH), and sodium hydroxide (NaO). Bases taste bitter, but you would not want to taste-test a base. Bases denature (damage) proteins, and proteins are what you are made of.

The Hydrogen Inside of You

You, your teacher, your dog, the trees in the park, the birds in the trees, the worms in the soil—every living creature contains hydrogen. In fact, there are about 1.6 ounces (45 grams) of hydrogen for every 1 pound (454 g) in a human being. So if you weigh 100 pounds (45 kilograms), you contain 10 pounds (4.5 kg) of hydrogen. With hydrogen making up about 10 percent of our bodies, it makes sense that it is called one of the building blocks of life. Other building blocks include carbon (C), oxygen, nitrogen, sulfur (S), and phosphorus (P). All of these elements combine easily with hydrogen.

Hydrogen Gets Heavy

One of the most interesting forms of hydrogen is its isotopes. An isotope of an element is an atom that has the same number of protons but a different number of neutrons. Hydrogen is the only element with names for its isotopes—protium (H), deuterium (D), and tritium (T). These three isotopes are different types of hydrogen.

Protium is the regular version of hydrogen and is represented by the letter H. Protium has one proton and no neutrons. Deuterium has one neutron and one proton—unlike the more common hydrogen atom, which has one proton, one electron, and no neutrons. Deuterium is called "heavy" hydrogen because of the extra weight of the neutron. Deuterium can combine with oxygen to form "heavy" water (D_2O). About one out of every 6,000 water molecules found naturally on Earth in oceans, lakes, and rivers contains deuterium.

Meanwhile, tritium has two neutrons. Tritium and oxygen often combine in the atmosphere and reach Earth as radioactive rain. There are two types of radiation: ionizing and non-ionizing. Ionization is where electrons are spontaneously emitted from an atom to create a very unstable substance, sometimes so unstable that it explodes. The electrons that leave the atom are very dangerous. They can damage living cells and are known to cause cancer. Non-ionizing radiation, such as what is experienced from heat, visible light, or radio waves, is not

Protium　　　　**Deuterium**　　　　**Tritium**

Hydrogen has three isotopes. Protium, which makes up ordinary hydrogen, has only one proton and no neutrons in its nucleus. Deuterium (^{2}H) is called heavy hydrogen because it has one proton and one neutron in its nucleus, doubling its atomic weight. Tritium (^{3}H) has one proton and two neutrons in its nucleus, tripling its atomic weight.

strong enough to cause electrons to be forced out. This radiation is not considered dangerous. Radioactive rain can contain both ionizing and non-ionizing radiation. However, this radioactivity decays quickly and does not build up.

Chapter Four
Hydrogen Hooks Up

Knowing that hydrogen can readily combine with other elements, let's take a look at these combinations, or compounds. Compounds can be made of two atoms, such as carbon monoxide (CO), with the formula of one carbon atom and one oxygen atom. We learned that water (H_2O) is a simple compound—two hydrogen atoms and one oxygen atom. But compounds can also be made up of a lot of atoms, such as hydroxyzine ($C_{21}H_{27}ClN_2O_2$)—a compound that is made up of twenty-one atoms of carbon, twenty-seven atoms of hydrogen, one atom of chlorine, two atoms of nitrogen, and two atoms of oxygen. Hydroxyzine is used as a tranquilizer, a drug that causes sleepiness, and also as an antihistamine, a drug that helps stop your runny nose when you are suffering from a cold or allergy.

Hydrogen Peroxide

Hydrogen combines with oxygen to make water, but it also teams up with oxygen to form another bubblier compound. If you have ever fallen down on the sidewalk and scraped your knee, then you have probably experienced the compound of two hydrogen atoms and two oxygen atoms—H_2O_2. This compound is hydrogen peroxide. In its most watered-down state, hydrogen peroxide is the bubbly disinfectant that

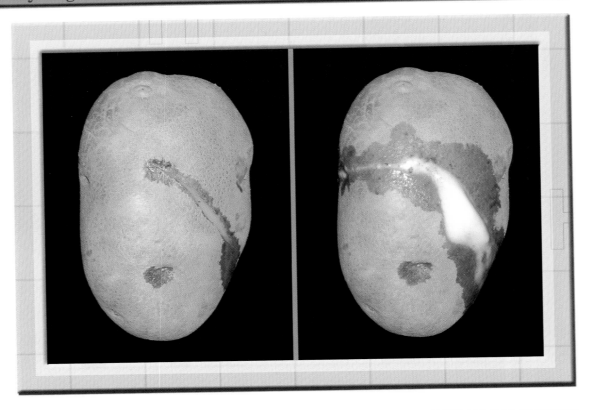

The chemical reaction of hydrogen peroxide on damaged human skin can be reproduced with a common potato. Both human skin and potatoes contain an enzyme, or protein, called a catalase. When a potato is cut with a knife *(left)*, there are a lot of catalases floating around the damaged section. When hydrogen peroxide is poured on the cut, the catalases break the hydrogen apart into a foamy mixture of water and oxygen *(right)*. On human skin, this reaction will help clean the wound.

fights germs and is often found in first aid kits. It helps cuts and scrapes heal better.

Hydrogen peroxide will also bleach items, so you don't want to spill it on your clothes! Some hair-lightening kits contain hydrogen peroxide, and sometimes the chemical will cause hair to turn more of a brassy orange than the blond color that was intended. In highly concentrated solutions, hydrogen peroxide can be found in rocket fuel. H_2O_2 is pretty amazing—not only can it turn your hair orange, but it can also shoot you into space!

Hydrogen Sulfide

While hydrogen by itself does not have an odor, when it combines with sulfur you can definitely smell it—but you wouldn't want to! Hydrogen sulfide (H_2S) is flammable, smells like rotten eggs, and is found in mineral waters, volcanic gases, and decaying matter. In fact, the decaying matter in your stomach can create hydrogen sulfide gas, which can be expelled as flatulence.

Hydrogen Cyanide

Another hydrogen compound that also has an odor is hydrogen cyanide (HCN). This poisonous and deadly compound smells like almonds. Hydrogen cyanide can be found in the production of fuel from coal. The compound can also be used to make plastic. If you've ever eaten a whole peach and have been left with just the pit, also called a stone, then you've been in contact with naturally occurring HCN. But don't worry, it is perfectly safe in peaches—just don't try to eat the pit.

Hydrogenation

Besides providing us with something to drink or making sure a cut doesn't get infected, hydrogen is also used to process food. Processed food is treated or prepared food using artifical means.

Whenever you spread margarine on your toast, you're getting ready to eat a result of the process called hydrogenation. The hydrogenation process works like this: When hydrogen is added to the double bonds of carbon found in animal fat or vegetable oil molecules, it hardens those molecules. This hardening makes it possible for a stick of margarine to sit on the dining table and not turn into a plate of yellow ooze. But if you've ever seen the gooey mess that happens if you accidentally leave

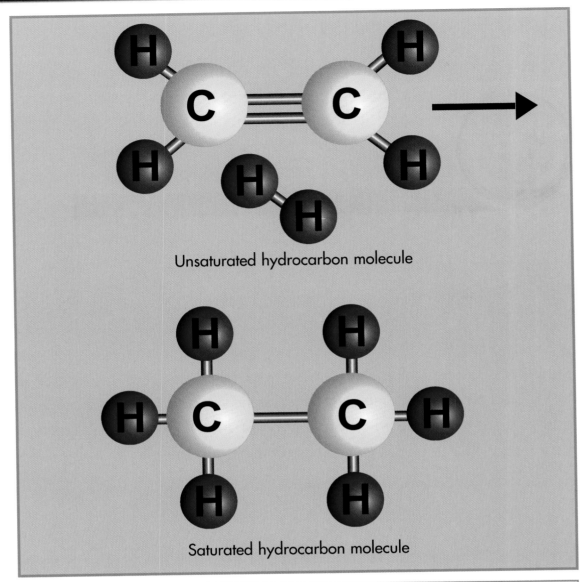

Unsaturated hydrocarbon molecule

Saturated hydrocarbon molecule

Hydrogenation occurs when hydrogen atoms are added to unsaturated hydro-carbon molecules, which have room to add more atoms. Ethene *(top)* has a double covalent bond, which is the sharing of electrons between two atoms. Ethene is an unsaturated hydrocarbon molecule and becomes saturated when an extra hydrogen molecule is added *(below)*, creating single covalent bonds.

margarine out for too long, then you know that the hardening of the molecules can be reversed by a rise in temperature.

Hydrogenation turns unsaturated fats into partially saturated ones because they are saturated by hydrogen. Saturated fat, also called

Many foods you eat contain partially hydrogenated oils. Foods such as french fries are fried in hydrogenated oils. Health officials say that consuming too many foods with hydrogenated oil can lead to heart disease.

trans fat or partially hydrogenated oil, is very common in nearly all the foods people like to eat, such as french fries, cookies, and potato chips. Anytime you see "partially hydrogenated oil" listed in the ingredients, you know that food contains saturated fat. Although saturated fat makes foods tasty, it has also been linked to heart disease and other illnesses. Food companies are experimenting with ways to create the foods people love without using saturated fat. In 2002, Frito-Lay, the maker of Doritos and Cheetos, was one of the food companies that introduced new snacks that did not contain trans fats.

But examples of hydrogenation aren't just found in vending machines—the process is also used to create high-grade gasoline. This occurs when large molecules are broken down into smaller molecules and react with hydrogen.

Carbohydrates

In addition to hydrogenation, hydrogen can also bond with carbon and oxygen in a different process to create other fuels for our bodies called carbohydrates. These are any of the starches or sugars found in foods, especially in vegetables like corn and potatoes. Because pasta and bread come from plants like wheat, these foods also contain carbohydrates. Carbohydrates always contain carbon, hydrogen, and oxygen.

Carbohydrates are created during a natural chemical process called photosynthesis. This is when a plant absorbs carbon dioxide (CO_2) from the air, combines it with the water it receives from its roots, and transforms it into either sugar

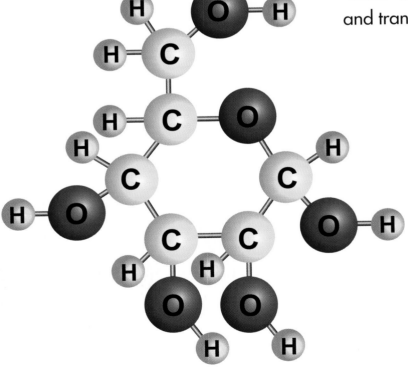

Carbohydrates are made during the process of photosynthesis. At left is a model for a sugar known as glucose, one of the simplest carbohydrates. In your body, glucose flows in your bloodstream and is absorbed through cell walls to be converted into energy that your body uses.

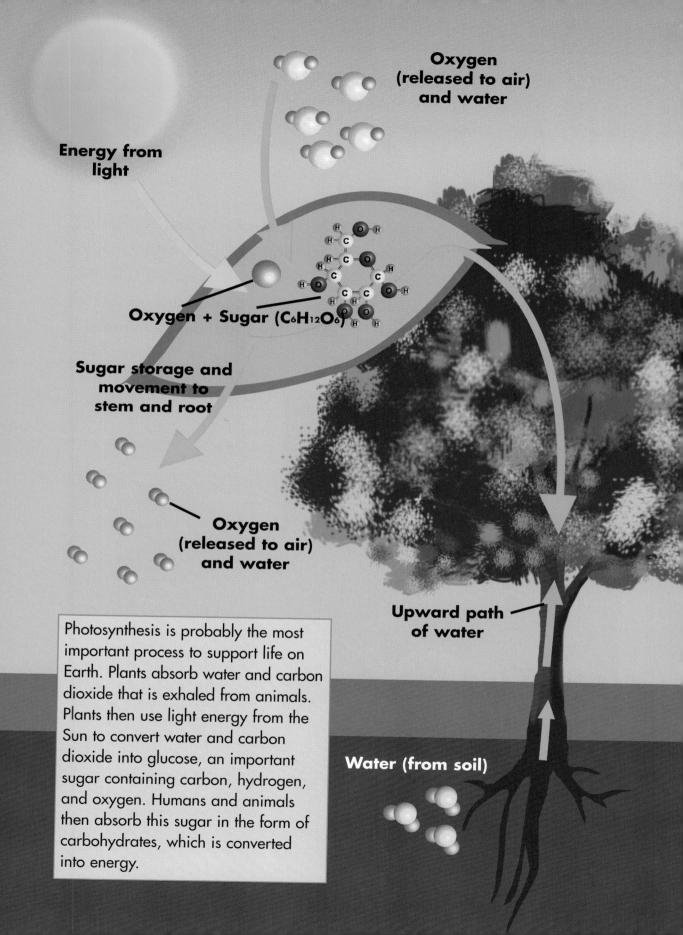

Oxygen (released to air) and water

Energy from light

Oxygen + Sugar (C₆H₁₂O₆)

$Oxygen + Sugar (C_6H_{12}O_6)$

Sugar storage and movement to stem and root

Oxygen (released to air) and water

Upward path of water

Photosynthesis is probably the most important process to support life on Earth. Plants absorb water and carbon dioxide that is exhaled from animals. Plants then use light energy from the Sun to convert water and carbon dioxide into glucose, an important sugar containing carbon, hydrogen, and oxygen. Humans and animals then absorb this sugar in the form of carbohydrates, which is converted into energy.

Water (from soil)

$(C_6H_{12}O_6)$ or starch $(C_6H_{10}O_5)$. Foods rich in carbohydrates, such as potatoes and pasta, provide a lot of energy to the body. Many athletes will stock up on carbohydrates the night before a big competition.

Hydrocarbons

The combination of hydrogen and carbon can not only fuel our bodies, but it can also provide the energy that runs our cars and provides electricity for our homes. The chemical compound is called a hydrocarbon, and its chemical symbol varies depending on the number of atoms combining to form each molecule. For instance, methane is a hydrocarbon and its symbol is CH_4. Propane, another hydrocarbon,

Hydrogen is found almost everywhere—even in your backyard. Many outdoor grills are fueled by propane, a hydrocarbon. Hydrocarbons occur naturally and are often found in fossil fuels such as natural gas, coal, and petroleum. Hydrogen fuel cells are being developed to be used as a renewable source of energy. A hydrogen fuel cell works similarly to the way a battery does, except that it won't run down as long as hydrogen is provided. These fuel cells would be a cleaner source of energy than the fossil fuels currently being used.

Hydrogen gas is produced during a chemical reaction between aluminum (Al) and sodium hydroxide (NaOH). Aluminum foil is placed in a beaker containing water (H_2O) and sodium hydroxide *(photo 1)*, a base. The base reacts with the aluminum *(photo 2)* and produces hydrogen gas (H_2). Soon, enough hydrogen gas is produced to blow up a balloon *(photo 3)*.

has the chemical symbol C_3H_8. These hydrocarbons are found in petroleum, natural gas, and coal, which are used to fuel many mechanical engines.

When you ride in a car, a bus, or a plane, you are experiencing the energy of hydrogen. As combustion, or heat, is applied to gas, the hydrocarbon molecules break apart, causing energy to be released. In fact, hydrogen makes a popping noise when it is burned. This happens because a lot of energy is released. This energy appears in the form of heat, light, or sound.

Hydrocarbons, carbohydrates, hydrogen peroxide—these are just a few of the compounds that are created when hydrogen combines with other elements. If you look up "hydro" or "hydrogen" in the dictionary, look at the words that follow and you'll learn about other compounds that contain hydrogen, such as hydrocortisone, hydrogen bromide, and hydrogen fluoride, to name a few.

Chapter Five
Hydrogen Flexes Its Muscles

Now that we've learned how hydrogen can be used to create energy, let's look to the sky for some additional inspiration. We learned in chapter three that the Sun is mostly one big ball of hydrogen and that hydrogen is flammable. But why does the Sun shine? Scientists, most notably Albert Einstein, were puzzled by this question for centuries. It was several decades after Einstein created the equation $E=mc^2$ in the early 1900s that scientists realized why this great ball of fire burns so bright.

Around 1915, Einstein published a paper explaining what he called the theory of relativity, or $E=mc^2$. Prior to Einstein's equation, scientists thought that energy (E) and mass (m) were unrelated. Through a series of mathematical processes, Einstein revealed that mass and energy are equal when you take the speed of light by itself. The American Museum of Natural History (AMNH) gives a great example: if you took a small piece of mass, such as a penny, and multiplied it by the speed of light squared (c^2), the energy it would release would be huge. If we could convert the mass of a penny to energy, it would be enough energy to power New York City for at least two years. "Changing a penny entirely to energy would require temperatures and pressures much greater than those found inside the sun. So, unfortunately, small coins are not a practical source of energy," explains the AMNH.

The Theory of Relativity

Let's look at Einstein's famous theory a little more closely:

E Energy

m Mass (a property of matter)

c Speed of light (186,282 miles per second, or 299,792 kilometers per second); the speed at which light travels in a vacuum, which is an area without any matter

2 Squared (a number multiplied by itself)

German physicist Albert Einstein works out an equation on a blackboard in 1931. Einstein's theory of relativity explains the relationship between mass and energy. Later, scientists learned how to turn the mass of a hydrogen atom into energy. The result was the hydrogen bomb, one of the most destructive devices man has ever built.

Hydrogen into Helium

So what does $E=mc^2$ actually mean? In order to answer this, we must first learn about fusion. When four hydrogen atoms bang into each other, they eventually will fuse together to form a single helium atom. These collisions and the joining together of elements that result are called fusion. This process of fusion to form helium releases a lot of energy, which causes the Sun to burn so hot. The theory of relativity explains how energy is released from fusion—enormous amounts of mass under a lot of pressure and extremely high temperatures create energy. According to the AMNH, fusion occurs on the Sun "100 million

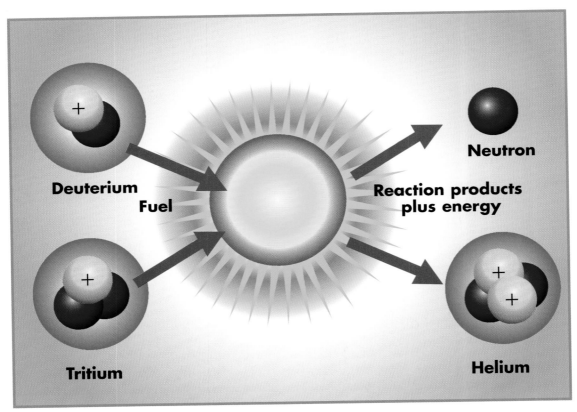

Fusion occurs when two lighter nuclei join together to form one heavier nucleus. The deuterium-tritium reaction *(above)* is a simple form of fusion often used in nuclear reactors to produce energy. In this reaction, hydrogen isotopes deuterium and tritium slam together to produce helium and massive amounts of energy.

quadrillion quadrillion times each second, and the Sun has enough hydrogen to continue burning for another five billion years."

Hydrogen Becomes a Bomb

In the 1950s, American scientists attempted to harness the Sun's energy when they invented the hydrogen bomb. The United States had already made the atom bomb, which was dropped on the cities of Hiroshima and Nagasaki, Japan, during World War II (1939–1945). These atom bombs were devastating, killing hundreds of thousands of people and essentially ending the war.

Dubbed the H-bomb, the hydrogen bomb would be even more powerful. The atom bomb and other similar bombs used fission—the process of splitting atoms. The hydrogen bomb uses fusion, much like the Sun does, to create enormous amounts of energy. Just how much energy this bomb contained would be seen in 1952, when it was dropped on a small island in the Pacific Ocean during an experiment. This bomb was 700 times more powerful than the atomic bomb that was dropped on Hiroshima. During the experiment, the H-bomb completely vaporized this island that had previously measured 1 mile (1.6 km) in diameter. It would take more than 1 million tons of dynamite to make a blast that big. According to reports of those who witnessed the blast, the bomb created a fireball that was 3 miles (5 km) wide, and a gigantic mushroom cloud rose from the blast in just 90 seconds. The power of the Sun had been harnessed that day and would change world politics forever. Today, several countries, including the United States, possess hydrogen bombs.

Hydrogen as Clean Energy

Aside from bombs, though, scientists are also developing ways to harness the power of hydrogen to create a cleaner form of energy.

Gasoline and other fossil fuels that we use as energy sources pollute the air. Several car manufacturers have already built hydrogen-powered cars and are rolling them out to customers. Along with hydrogen being a clean energy source, it is also recyclable. In other words, you can use parts of it again and again, unlike fossil fuels, such as natural gas or coal, which are available only in a limited amount.

Recycling Hydrogen

The hydrogen cycle shows how hydrogen can be cleanly used and reused. The hydrogen cycle starts with water, which is then split apart into

Scientists used fusion to harness the power of the Sun. Here, a hydrogen bomb is tested on Bikini Atoll, an island in the South Pacific, in 1952. The force of the bomb vaporized the entire island. The development of the hydrogen bomb was a direct result of the arms race between the United States and the former Soviet Union.

hydrogen and oxygen by using electrolysis. The oxygen is then released into the air, but the hydrogen is captured and contained in a fuel cell, which stores energy. These fuel cells can power everything from a school bus to an airplane to a space shuttle. However, unlike cars and planes that run on fossil fuels, when the hydrogen fuel cells are used in these machines, they create very little and sometimes no pollution. The main thing that is released from these fuel cells is water, which can then be split into hydrogen and oxygen, and the hydrogen can be used all over again. Being able to recycle hydrogen may change the way we live.

Hydrogen Is One Cool Gas

Because of the hydrogen bomb, the Sun, the *Hindenburg*, and all the fuels derived from hydrogen, it is easy to think only of fire when we think of this element. But hydrogen can also be found in a very cold form—liquid hydrogen. Liquid hydrogen is so incredibly cold that if you were to place a tennis ball in a bowl of liquid hydrogen, take it out, and then immediately bounce it on the ground, the ball would shatter like glass.

Liquid hydrogen is used in cryogenics, which is the study of the effects of very cold temperatures. The National Aeronautics and Space Administration (NASA) is one agency that is studying cryogenics. For example, when a space shuttle, satellite, or other spacecraft is returning to Earth from space, it is moving at a tremendous speed. Entering Earth's atmosphere at tremendous speeds can create extremely high temperatures, which could severely damage the spacecraft. Cryogenics can help engineers and other researchers learn how to properly cool down such vessels during reentry.

At the NASA Goddard Space Flight Center in Greenbelt, Maryland, scientists are using cryogenics to observe stars. According to NASA's Web site, "Sensitive sensors can catch even the weakest signals

LIQUIFIED HYDROGEN
FLAMMABLE GAS

NASA uses liquid hydrogen to power its spacecraft, such as the space shuttle *Discovery*, pictured here in 1999. Liquid hydrogen, which is stored at temperatures less than -400°F (-240°C), offers a massive energy resource that doesn't require the ship to carry too much fuel.

reaching us from the stars. Many of these sensors must be cooled well below room temperature to have the necessary sensitivity."

Be a Sun Worshipper

The Sun is made of the same elements as all the other stars in the universe—hydrogen and helium. The Sun is estimated to be 4.6 billion years old and is so large that more than a million Earths could fit inside of it.

In about 5 billion years, the Sun is expected to run out of fuel. It will become another type of star called a red giant. The Sun will then become 100 times bigger than its current size. The heat it will give off will completely burn up Mercury, Venus, and Earth. After that, the Sun will lose its outer gas layers and all that will remain is another type of star called a white dwarf. As a white dwarf, the Sun will be about the size of Earth, but it will be white hot, hence the name. Eventually, it will begin to cool and then just disappear.

In this book, you learned that hydrogen is a flammable, colorless, odorless, and extremely light element that can be found as a gas and is most commonly found in water. But now that you know so much about the role of hydrogen in our daily lives, you'll be amazed at how many other places you'll find hydrogen. Whether it's the Sun shining in the sky, cars driving down the road, or even the spaghetti on your dinner plate, hydrogen is the power provider for the entire universe.

The Periodic Table of Elements

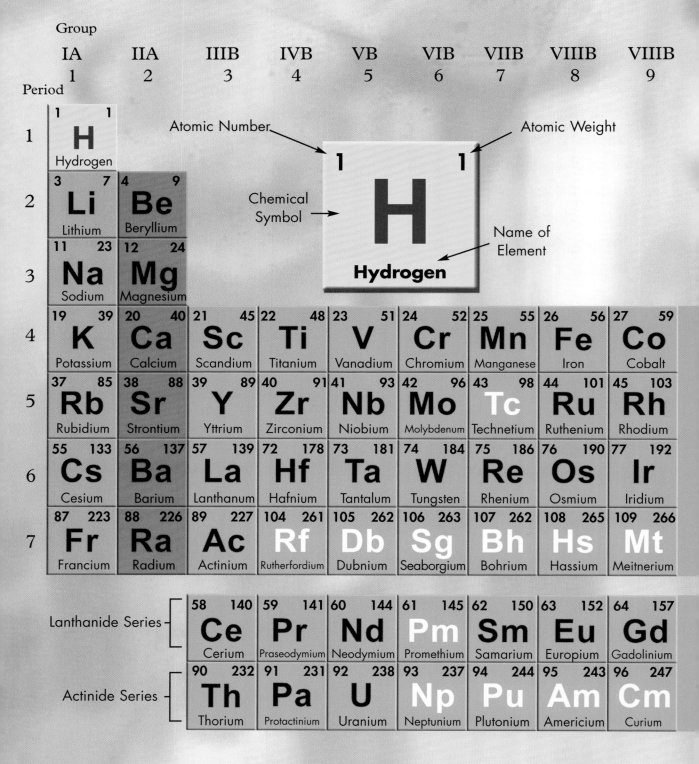

Group

| IA 1 | IIA 2 | IIIB 3 | IVB 4 | VB 5 | VIB 6 | VIIB 7 | VIIIB 8 | VIIIB 9 |

Period

Atomic Number

Atomic Weight

Chemical Symbol

1	1
	H
	Hydrogen

Name of Element

1

1	1							
H Hydrogen								
2 3 7 **Li** Lithium	4 9 **Be** Beryllium							
3 11 23 **Na** Sodium	12 24 **Mg** Magnesium							
4 19 39 **K** Potassium	20 40 **Ca** Calcium	21 45 **Sc** Scandium	22 48 **Ti** Titanium	23 51 **V** Vanadium	24 52 **Cr** Chromium	25 55 **Mn** Manganese	26 56 **Fe** Iron	27 59 **Co** Cobalt
5 37 85 **Rb** Rubidium	38 88 **Sr** Strontium	39 89 **Y** Yttrium	40 91 **Zr** Zirconium	41 93 **Nb** Niobium	42 96 **Mo** Molybdenum	43 98 **Tc** Technetium	44 101 **Ru** Ruthenium	45 103 **Rh** Rhodium
6 55 133 **Cs** Cesium	56 137 **Ba** Barium	57 139 **La** Lanthanum	72 178 **Hf** Hafnium	73 181 **Ta** Tantalum	74 184 **W** Tungsten	75 186 **Re** Rhenium	76 190 **Os** Osmium	77 192 **Ir** Iridium
7 87 223 **Fr** Francium	88 226 **Ra** Radium	89 227 **Ac** Actinium	104 261 **Rf** Rutherfordium	105 262 **Db** Dubnium	106 263 **Sg** Seaborgium	107 262 **Bh** Bohrium	108 265 **Hs** Hassium	109 266 **Mt** Meitnerium

Lanthanide Series	58 140 **Ce** Cerium	59 141 **Pr** Praseodymium	60 144 **Nd** Neodymium	61 145 **Pm** Promethium	62 150 **Sm** Samarium	63 152 **Eu** Europium	64 157 **Gd** Gadolinium
Actinide Series	90 232 **Th** Thorium	91 231 **Pa** Protactinium	92 238 **U** Uranium	93 237 **Np** Neptunium	94 244 **Pu** Plutonium	95 243 **Am** Americium	96 247 **Cm** Curium

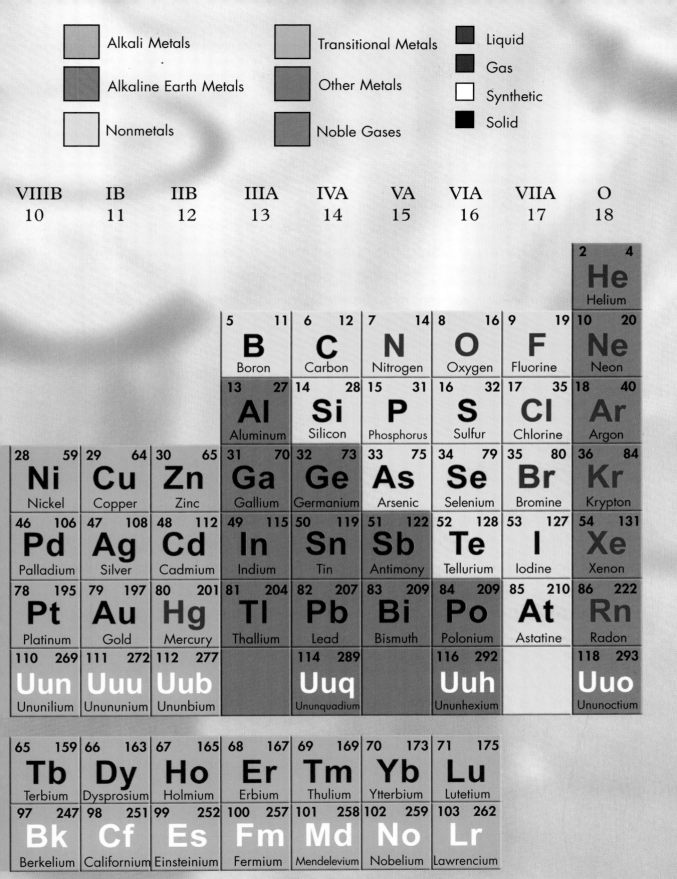

Alkali Metals

Alkaline Earth Metals

Nonmetals

Transitional Metals

Other Metals

Noble Gases

Liquid

Gas

Synthetic

Solid

VIIIB 10	IB 11	IIB 12	IIIA 13	IVA 14	VA 15	VIA 16	VIIA 17	O 18
								2 4 **He** Helium
			5 11 **B** Boron	6 12 **C** Carbon	7 14 **N** Nitrogen	8 16 **O** Oxygen	9 19 **F** Fluorine	10 20 **Ne** Neon
			13 27 **Al** Aluminum	14 28 **Si** Silicon	15 31 **P** Phosphorus	16 32 **S** Sulfur	17 35 **Cl** Chlorine	18 40 **Ar** Argon
28 59 **Ni** Nickel	29 64 **Cu** Copper	30 65 **Zn** Zinc	31 70 **Ga** Gallium	32 73 **Ge** Germanium	33 75 **As** Arsenic	34 79 **Se** Selenium	35 80 **Br** Bromine	36 84 **Kr** Krypton
46 106 **Pd** Palladium	47 108 **Ag** Silver	48 112 **Cd** Cadmium	49 115 **In** Indium	50 119 **Sn** Tin	51 122 **Sb** Antimony	52 128 **Te** Tellurium	53 127 **I** Iodine	54 131 **Xe** Xenon
78 195 **Pt** Platinum	79 197 **Au** Gold	80 201 **Hg** Mercury	81 204 **Tl** Thallium	82 207 **Pb** Lead	83 209 **Bi** Bismuth	84 209 **Po** Polonium	85 210 **At** Astatine	86 222 **Rn** Radon
110 269 **Uun** Ununilium	111 272 **Uuu** Unununium	112 277 **Uub** Ununbium		114 289 **Uuq** Ununquadium		116 292 **Uuh** Ununhexium		118 293 **Uuo** Ununoctium

65 159 **Tb** Terbium	66 163 **Dy** Dysprosium	67 165 **Ho** Holmium	68 167 **Er** Erbium	69 169 **Tm** Thulium	70 173 **Yb** Ytterbium	71 175 **Lu** Lutetium
97 247 **Bk** Berkelium	98 251 **Cf** Californium	99 252 **Es** Einsteinium	100 257 **Fm** Fermium	101 258 **Md** Mendelevium	102 259 **No** Nobelium	103 262 **Lr** Lawrencium

Glossary

atom   The smallest, most basic unit of an element; made up of protons, neutrons, and electrons.

atomic number   The number of protons in the nucleus of an atom, which is usually equal to the number of electrons.

atomic weight   The mass of one atom of an element.

combustion   A chemical process that produces heat, energy, and often light.

cryogenics   The study of extremely low temperatures.

diatomic   Consisting of two atoms of the same element.

electron   A negatively charged particle outside an atom's nucleus.

element   The basic matter that all things are made of; any matter made up of one kind of atom.

fission   The splitting of an atomic nucleus.

flammable   Capable of catching fire easily.

fusion   The coming together of atomic nuclei to form heavier nuclei, resulting in the production of large amounts of energy.

hydrogenation   The process of adding hydrogen to a molecule; often used in producing food.

molecule   The smallest bit of matter before it gets broken down into its basic parts, or atoms.

neutron   A particle within the nucleus of an atom that contains no charge; found in the nucleus of all elements except hydrogen.

nucleus   The positively charged central portion of an atom.

period   A horizontal row in the periodic table; also called a row.

photosynthesis   Formation of carbohydrates from carbon dioxide and hydrogen.

proton   A positively charged particle within the nucleus of an atom. The number of protons and electrons is almost always equal.

American Museum of Natural History
Central Park West at 79th Street
New York, NY 10024
(212) 769-5000

Los Alamos National Laboratory
P.O. Box 1663
Los Alamos, NM 87545
(505) 667-7000

National Hydrogen Association
1800 M Street NW, Suite 300
Washington, DC 20036
(202) 223-5547

Web Sites

Due to the changing nature of Internet links, the Rosen Publishing Group, Inc., has developed an online list of Web sites related to the subject of this book. This site is updated regularly. Please use this link to access the list:

http://www.rosenlinks.com/uept/hydr

For Further Reading

Gardner, Robert. *Kitchen Chemistry*. New York: Simon & Schuster, 1988.

Strathern, Paul. *Mendeleyev's Dream: The Quest for the Elements*. New York: St. Martin's Press, 2001.

Stwertka, Albert. *A Guide to the Elements*. 2nd Edition. New York: Oxford University Press, 2002.

Bibliography

American Hydrogen Association. Retrieved August 2003 (http://www.clean-air.org).

American Museum of Natural History. Retrieved August 2003 (http://www.amnh.org).

Harvard School of Public Health. Retrieved September 2003 (http://www.hsph.harvard.edu).

Hydrogen Energy Center. Retrieved September 2003 (http://www.h2eco.org).

MadSci Network. Retrieved August 2003 (http://www.madsci.org).

"Periodic Table." Los Alamos National Laboratory. Retrieved August 2003 (http://pearl1.lanl.gov).

Stwertka, Albert. *A Guide to the Elements*. 2nd Edition. New York: Oxford University Press, 2002.

"Web Element's Periodic Table." Web Elements Ltd. Retrieved August 2003 (http://www.webelements.com).

Index

About the Author

Linda Saucerman is an editor and writer living in Brooklyn, New York, with her husband and their dog and cat.

Photo Credits

Cover, pp. 1, 10, 11, 15, 16, 21, 24, 26, 28, 30, 31, 36 by Tahara Hasan; pp. 5, 8, 35 © Bettmann/Corbis; p. 17 © Archives Larousse, Paris, France/Bridgeman Art Library; p. 18 © Steve Raymer/Corbis; p. 20 © David A. Hardy/Photo Researchers, Inc.; pp. 29, 40 © AP/Wide World Photos; p. 32 © Sonda Dawes/The Image Works; p. 33 by Maura McConnell; p. 38 © Martin Bond/Photo Researchers, Inc.

Special thanks to Rosemarie Allen and Westtown School, in Westtown, Pennsylvania.

Designer: Tahara Hasan; Editor: Charles Hofer